GLOBAL ORGANIZAT

# The World Health Organization

A+
**Smart Apple Media**

Smart Apple Media is published by Black Rabbit Books
P.O. Box 3263, Mankato, Minnesota 56002

Printed in Hong Kong

Designed by Helen James
Edited by Mary-Jane Wilkins
Picture research by Su Alexander

Library of Congress Cataloging-in-Publication Data

Connolly, Sean, 1956–
The World Health Organization / Sean Connolly.
    p. cm.—(Smart Apple Media. Global organizations)
    Summary: "Describes the historical and current efforts of the World Health
Organization to ensure that everyone has access to health care and the efforts of
the organization to contain communicable diseases"—Provided by publisher.
    Includes index.
    ISBN 978-1-59920-302-7
  1.  World Health Organization—Juvenile literature. 2.  Public health—International
cooperation—Juvenile literature. 3.  World health—Juvenile literature.  I. Title.
RA8.C53 2009
362.1—dc22
                                                          2007038994


Photograph acknowledgements
Page 6 Patrick Robert/Corbis; 8 Hulton-Deutsch Collection/Corbis;
10 & 11 Bettmann/Corbis; 13 Hulton Deutsch Collection/Corbis;
15 WHO; 17 Bettmann/Corbis; 18 Corbis; 20 Bettmann/Corbis; 21 WHO;
22 Peter Turnley/Corbis; 25 China Photo/Reuters/Corbis; 27 Mian Khursheed/
Reuters/Corbis; 28 Stephanie Sinclair/Corbis; 29 Chaiwat Subprasom/Reuters/
Corbis; Viviane Moos/Corbis; 32 Dominique Derda/France 2/Corbis; 33 Gideon
Mendel/Corbis; 35 Antony Njuguna/Reuters/Corbis; 36 Reuters/Corbis;
37 Kin Cheung/Reuters/Corbis; 38 WHO; 39 Grothe/D.M.N./Corbis Sygma;
41 WHO/P.Virot; 43 WHO
Front cover Patrick Robert/Corbis

9 8 7 6 5 4 3 2 1

# CONTENTS

# The Health of the World

**More than 6.6 billion people** live in the world today—more than double the number there were 40 years ago. In that time, there have been many advances in the fields of science and technology (cell phones, high-definition TV, and the Internet). Yet many of those 6.6 billion people live in conditions that have worsened during the past 40 years.

*A WHO clinic in Mali collects blood from children to test for African human trypanosomiasis. This deadly disease, also known as sleeping sickness, has become common again in many parts of Africa.*

Some age-old diseases, such as malaria, pneumonia, and tuberculosis, remain common in many parts of the world and kill millions of people every year. Other diseases, such as HIV/AIDS and SARS, seem to come from nowhere and become killers overnight. All of these illnesses, new and old, sweep through poorer parts of the world. Meanwhile, people in richer countries continue to harm themselves by smoking, eating unhealthily, and exercising little or not at all.

The World Health Organization (WHO) is the United Nations' special agency for health. It deals with all of these health issues and tries to find world solutions to world problems. The WHO has a simple aim—to improve people's health and well-being. But this is never simple or straightforward, and the WHO is often on the front line of many battles.

## Enough To Eat?

If all the food produced in the world today were distributed equally, every person would be able to consume 2,760 calories a day. The WHO defines hunger as consuming fewer than 1,960 calories a day. By that definition, United Nations' sources estimate that there are more than 850 million permanently hungry people in the world today.

## ... ON THE SCENE ... ON THE SCENE ... ON THE SCENE ...

### A Sense of Accomplishment
*The people involved with WHO, from the most senior directors to those who transport medicines by bicycle, share a sense of doing something useful. They know the scale of the problem of world health but share the feeling of joy and brotherhood that comes from helping others.*

*Dr. Wildred Nkhoma, from the African country of Malawi, is part of the WHO effort to tackle epidemics and tuberculosis in Africa. His views about the WHO and its role are shared by many others: "Working for WHO means being a servant for those who can benefit from what you know, even if they may not know that you exist."*

# Harnessing Hope

## During the nineteenth century,

there were many advances, including the telegraph and telephone, and the spread of railways and steam-powered ships. Clothes, furniture, and tools could be produced in large quantities and sold cheaply across the globe.

For many people, this Industrial Revolution brought new comfort and wealth. For others, however, progress led to sickness and death. Living conditions were desperate for many who worked in the new factories in the United States and other developed countries.

*A representative of the Barnardo's charity visits a family in an East London slum in 1916. The charity's founder, Dr. Thomas Barnardo, helped poor and sick young people in British cities.*

Overcrowded slums with bad sanitation became breeding grounds for killer diseases such as typhus and cholera, which already affected millions of people throughout the world.

## The Wider World

At the same time, there were reasons to be optimistic. The nineteenth century was a time of great medical progress, when scientists developed new equipment and treatments to fight disease. They were eager to share their findings. In 1851, representatives from 12 countries met in Paris to discuss ways to control the spread of disease. Later conferences led to more ambitious aims. For example, the scientists exchanged the latest information on specific treatments.

By 1907, the world medical community had established the first international organization devoted to public health. Based in Paris, it was called the Office International d'Hygiène Publique (International Office for Public Health, known by its French abbreviation OIHP). The OIHP grew quickly from 12 members to 60 in its first seven years. But then it suspended work because World War I began in Europe.

That war led to the death of about ten million people. But millions more died after the fighting ended in November 1918. A wave of influenza, or flu, followed in the tracks of soldiers returning from the fighting. From 1918–19, between 15 and 20 million people died from influenza around the world. Some medical sources now believe that as many as 50 million to 100 million people died from this flu pandemic.

## Silver Lining

The terrible cost of World War I led international leaders to consider ways of preventing such bloodshed in the future. Within a year they had created the League of Nations, a world organization designed to reduce conflict and to promote peace.

## Influenza in 1918

*The strain of influenza that swept across the world in 1918 probably originated in Europe and spread among soldiers in camps and field hospitals. Soldiers and sailors returned to their homes after the war ended in November. Even the healthy among them carried germs that spread the influenza infection across the world.*

*The New Zealand Ministry for Culture and Heritage interviewed people who had lived through World War I and the influenza epidemic. A woman interviewee remembered hearing trucks making their way to the cemeteries daily (and nightly) at the time: "At night time was, I think, the saddest of all because the trucks were rumbling past my place all night long. We found out after that they didn't have time to make coffins; they were just buried in boxes, and the sad part was when we went over to the cemetery later, when it was all over, no one knew where they were putting the flowers. They just put them on a mound of ground and trusted the luck of it being one of their own."*

*A New York street cleaner wearing a face mask in 1918. People went to great lengths to avoid being infected with influenza.*

The millions of flu deaths that followed the war also affected the world community. In addition, typhus was sweeping through Poland and Russia. The OIHP lacked the resources to fight these major threats, so the League of Nations Health Organization was formed.

The obvious answer was to combine the health organization with the OIHP to form one international group that could act as the central information point for all medical and health issues in the world. Unfortunately, this did not happen. The U.S. was already the most powerful country in the world and could contribute greatly to any health organization, but it never joined the League of Nations (although it continued to belong to the OIHP). The two organizations remained separate, which weakened the chances of establishing a single health office for the world. A united organization would come, but not until there had been another global conflict.

*Typhus patients line the fence surrounding a Red Cross hospital in Estonia in the early 1920s. This deadly disease, spread by lice, swept through eastern Europe in the years following World War I. Many of the victims were soldiers.*

11

# Real Leadership

**Just more than 20 years** after the end of World War I, another global conflict began. The death toll from the fighting in World War II was far greater than in World War I. About 60 million people died, including 37 million civilians.

Once more, world leaders met and agreed that such a terrible war should never happen again. The United Nations, which celebrated its 60th birthday in 2005, was the result of the quest for world peace.

The UN plays a leading role in controlling conflicts throughout the world and in trying to restore peace to regions that have suffered from fighting and violence. But the UN does much more; it takes a longer (and broader) view of world events and tries to improve living conditions for everyone. The specialized agencies of the UN concentrate on different types of development, offering advice, practical help, equipment, and money to the neediest countries.

One of the most important UN agencies is the World Health Organization (WHO), which the UN established on April 7, 1948. The WHO aims to help all people achieve the highest standards of health possible. In this way, it is carrying on the work of the League of Nations Health Organization and the OIHP. However, it has a big advantage over these earlier groups: almost every country in the world is a member of the WHO, so the WHO has much more money for its projects.

## WHO Structure

Like its parent organization the UN, the WHO targets the whole world. No country is overlooked because of its political system, religious beliefs, or culture.

*A wounded American soldier attends mass on the Philippine island of Leyte during World War II. Millions of people around the world—soldiers and civilians alike—were wounded or killed during the six years of fighting.*

## The WHO Regions

WHO headquarters are in Geneva, Switzerland, but the organization does much of its work through regional and country offices around the world. Each of the 147 country offices is part of one of the six regional WHO offices (listed at right).

The regions have a great deal of independence in deciding on projects, in sending out emergency teams, and in using the money given to them by the wider WHO organization.

- European Region (office: Copenhagen, Denmark)
- Eastern Mediterranean Region (office: Cairo, Egypt)
- African Region (office: Brazzaville, Congo)
- Southeast Asian Region (office: New Delhi, India)
- Western Pacific Region (office: Manila, Philippines)
- Region of the Americas (office: Washington, D.C.)

And with only one or two exceptions, the WHO membership of 193 countries exactly matches the membership of the United Nations.

The World Health Organization is based in Geneva, Switzerland, which is the headquarters of many other European or international organizations. Each of its member states sends a representative to the WHO annual decision-making conference, known as the World Health Assembly. The assembly chooses the WHO's leader, or director-general (who serves for five years), and appoints a 32-member executive board.

The WHO's work in the field is carried out by a team of more than 8,000 health experts, including doctors, scientists, project managers, and other specialists. They are based in the 147 country offices, the most local of the WHO layers of organization.

## The Role of the WHO

Dr. Lee Jong-wook, the WHO's Director-General, who died suddenly in May 2006, defined the WHO's role as working for health. This aim echoes the central strategy of the organization since its beginning.

*WHO regional offices have more independence than many of their counterparts in other UN organizations. Each regional office decides on representatives to help make overall decisions in the World Health Assembly. This conference is based in WHO headquarters (right) in Geneva.*

The WHO constitution asserts that good health is a basic right: "Enjoyment of the highest attainable standard of health is one of the fundamental rights of every human being." The activities of the World Health Organization, Dr. Lee Jong-wook maintained, revolve around that basic statement.

## Important Changeover

When Director-General Dr. Lee Jong-wook died suddenly on May 22, 2006, the WHO executive board had to do some quick thinking. Could they wait nearly a year until the next World Health Assembly gathered before choosing Dr. Lee's successor? Would the world be satisfied with a temporary solution while avian flu, HIV/AIDS, and other health crises threatened?

The board decided to speed things up by calling a special meeting from November 6-8, 2006, followed by a one-day World Health Assembly on November 9. By November 8, they had narrowed down their choice for the job to one person—Dr. Margaret Chan of China. Dr. Chan has had a successful career in public health, first in Hong Kong, and then within WHO itself.

The assembly met on November 9, and agreed with the board's choice of successor. They appointed Dr. Chan as the next Director-General of the World Health Organization.

# First Line of Defense

**Several people** in a South American village become sick, running a high fever and feeling dizzy, light-headed, and incredibly thirsty. Within days, two of them have died. Reports come in of people with similar symptoms dying in neighboring villages.

No one can remember an illness that killed so quickly. People begin to panic. How far will this illness spread? Is everyone at risk? What can people do? This might sound like the opening scene from a science fiction film, but the idea of a killer disease racing through a region, country, or continent is not far-fetched. It happened with the Black Death in the Middle Ages and the spread of influenza in 1918–19.

## Ignorance and Delay

In previous centuries, people suffered and died in their own countries. The burden of caring for the sick and the dying fell on local people. Few people learned of advances in treatment of a disease in another

country, whether it was measles, whooping cough, or malaria. One reason for this is there were no real advances to announce.

Another reason was poor communication and the lack of a global health organization such as the WHO. For example, in 1747 the Scottish naval surgeon James Lind discovered that citrus fruits could help to prevent scurvy, a painful disease that particularly affected sailors. Britain's Royal Navy waited another 40 years before they acted on this information by carrying citrus fruit on every ship. Sailors from other countries had to wait even longer to hear the medical news.

*The Black Death swept through Europe in the fourteenth century. This engraving of the dead and the dying shows how it affected the Italian city of Florence.*

*The Cow-Pock — or — the Wonderful Effects of the New Inoculation! — Vide. the Publications of y Anti-Vaccine Society*

*The English artist James Gillray kept a shrewd eye on the world around him, giving us a glimpse of eighteenth- and nineteenth-century British life. This 1802 work pokes fun at the terror many people had of vaccination.*

## Sharing Medical Advances

Developments during the twentieth century showed how dangerous ignorance and inactivity could be. The sudden outbreak of a single disease—influenza—killed more people than a world war, which prompted the medical world to demand some form of information gathering and action. Today the World Health Organization plays such a role.

One of the most important roles for the World Health Organization is to pass on vital information about health and medicine. The founders of the WHO knew that in an age of frequent air travel, disease and infection can travel around the world in a matter of hours. But the information used to combat disease can travel much faster—at the speed of telephone or Internet connections.

The WHO can use its global network of offices to report news of diseases and to channel information about treatment to local people.

Many of the diseases tracked by the WHO—including diabetes, heart disease, and various forms of cancer—are limited to the sufferer and do not spread through a community or region. Others, such as HIV/AIDS and rapidly-changing forms of flu, can race from person to person very quickly.

One of the WHO's main defensive weapons is the Global Outbreak Alert and Response Network (see page 29), which is an international network of medical observers who send out alarms. This means that information about highly urgent threats, as well as anything that the WHO has tackled in the past, is available to the public.

## A Wealth of Information

The World Health Organization produces vast amounts of information about disease and health. This information is freely available to the public and to medical personnel around the world, so the WHO can continue its quest to improve health standards everywhere.

Health topics on the WHO website show just how detailed the WHO's efforts are. They range in alphabetical order from accidents to zoonoses (diseases which can be transmitted from animals to humans). The entries provide masses of information including what is being done, related links, WHO publications, and fact sheets.

Equipped with this information, doctors, nurses, and the general public can learn, for example, what chickenpox scabs look like, who is most at risk for measles, and how yellow fever got its name. Most importantly, accurate and detailed knowledge spreads across the world, which benefits everyone.

# Death of a Disease

Edward Jenner, an English country doctor who pioneered the technique of vaccination in the eighteenth century, wrote: "The annihilation of smallpox—the dreadful scourge of the human race—will be the final result of vaccination."

Jenner's prediction must have seemed unrealistic when he made it. At that time, one French person in ten died from the disease; even kings and queens became victims. As recently as 1967, 15 million to 20 million people worldwide suffered from the disease. Millions of them died or were permanently scarred.

In the same year, the World Health Organization launched its Intensified Smallpox Eradication Program. Using vaccination, medical staff had already wiped out smallpox across much of North America and Europe. The WHO program concentrated on developing countries, making it easier for local countries to develop and store vaccines. A new, easier-to-use needle made vaccination far more effective.

This program showed the WHO at its best, with local and regional teams who set their own targets. It also checked on results from around the world to pinpoint where more help was needed. One by one, countries began to report that smallpox had been eliminated within their borders. The last case of naturally occurring smallpox was reported in Somalia in 1977. The patient, a young man, survived. After a three-year period of observation (set by the WHO itself), smallpox was declared eradicated in 1980.

*This sculpture, by Italian Giulio Monteverde, shows Jenner vaccinating his son.*

## ... ON THE SCENE ... ON THE SCENE ... ON THE SCENE ...

### The Lionheart

*Since 1988, the World Health Organization has been working to wipe out polio in the same way it dealt with smallpox. The Global Polio Eradication Initiative relies on the same mix of central strategy and local efforts to succeed. And at the local level, WHO teams are winning support from some of the people who know most about polio—those who have had it themselves.*

*Isa Abdullahi plays goalie and coaches a youth soccer team in his native Nigeria, although he was severely crippled by polio when he was six.*

*Standing shakily on legs misshapen by the disease, he can still stop the hardest shots from opposing forwards. His bravery in the face of hardship has earned him the nickname "lionheart."*

*Isa is willing to make a similar effort to help the WHO's crusade against polio, especially in convincing families to have their children immunized against the disease. "Of course. If I have my way, I will be engaged in the immunization exercise. I am ready to go from house to house to carry out the exercise myself."*

# Global Warning

**The next time** you visit a doctor's office or health clinic, look around the waiting room. On many walls you will see posters offering advice about eating better, having your eyes tested, stopping smoking, or being checked for diseases such as diabetes.

Chances are there will also be leaflets and booklets to take with one or two Web sites mentioned. By offering this information, the doctor's office or clinic provides a public health service—spreading information about health and well-being and helping to prevent illnesses rather than just treat them. As a result of this information and advice, people in villages, towns, and cities are better off.

*War and illness go hand in hand. In the foreground are Rwandan victims of the disease cholera who died in a camp in Congo. Like thousands of other Rwandans, they had been forced to flee their country after a bloody civil war in 1994.*

The World Health Organization plays a similar role on a global scale. WHO staff, backed by a wealth of publications, programs, and Internet information, help to improve the living conditions of people all around the world. Much of the WHO information, such as warnings about drugs or poor diet, might be familiar to you. You may have heard similar messages from your parents, teachers, or doctor. But for many people in poorer, developing countries, receiving this information could mean the difference between life and death.

# International Health Regulations

The first meetings of international health officials in the nineteenth century, which led eventually to the formation of the WHO, came about as a result of the deadly cholera epidemics that swept across Europe between 1830 and 1847. Public health experts agreed that international cooperation in identifying such diseases and dealing with outbreaks was the only way to control epidemics in the future.

The World Health Organization continues with this aim through its International Health Regulations (IHR), which have been in place since 1969. At first, the IHR described six diseases as being notifiable. This means that member states must notify the WHO when they notice an outbreak. Having this information early on can help control the outbreak and prevent it from becoming more widespread.

The six notifiable diseases were

• cholera
• plague
• yellow fever
• smallpox
• relapsing fever
• typhus

Since then, the WHO and other health organizations have eliminated smallpox (see page 20) and gained increasing control over relapsing fever and typhus. Only cholera, plague, and yellow fever remain notifiable.

Since 2007, new measures have given the WHO more scope to gather information from member-states and to make demands of them.

# WHO Campaigns

The World Health Organization believes that keeping the public informed is just as important as treating illnesses. Unlike other international organizations, the WHO has many independent regional and local workers who can aim health messages at particular audiences.

This ability to target particular audiences is vital and effective. For example, advice offered to American or British people on how best to eat a balanced diet might offend villagers living in Bangladesh or Sudan.

WHO officials also understand how local societies operate. This understanding is especially important in passing on information about HIV/AIDS or other diseases that can be passed on sexually.

## ... ON THE SCENE ... ON THE SCENE ... ON THE SCENE ...

### The No-Smoking Village

*Hadji Abdallah, a radio reporter from Djibouti in east Africa, witnessed a great deal of violence when his country plunged into civil war in 1991. The upheaval badly affected people's health and well-being. So Abdallah established the "peace village" of Gallamo on abandoned ground. He wanted the village to be an example that other villages in Djibouti could follow.*

*The WHO was the first outside agency to help with the Gallamo project, offering Abdallah and other villagers money, helping to build a reservoir with clean water, and providing water pipes. This aid came from WHO funds for basic development needs. But Abdullah was keen to show that Gallamo could be more than simply a functioning new village. He concentrated on making it a beacon of good health as well.*

*The clean water supply has helped to end the threat of malaria (carried by mosquitoes that live in stagnant water). Gallamo villagers have agreed to ban smoking and the sale of tobacco. Just 15 years after Gallamo was founded, almost 350 families live in the village and the surrounding area. And with Djibouti's civil war now a fading memory, their children are growing up in a peaceful, healthy environment.*

## WHAT DO YOU THINK?

### A Moral Code?

*Some religious leaders believe that it is immoral to encourage people to have sex outside marriage. They argue that following a moral code—rather than using safe sex methods supported by the WHO—is the way to combat HIV/AIDS. What do you think?*

*A medical worker in full protective clothing enters a ward marked "contaminated area" in a hospital in southern China in early 2004. The deadly flu-like disease SARS threatened southeast Asia at the time.*

# Rapid Response

**Natural disasters** such as the Indian Ocean tsunami in December 2004 or the 2005 earthquake in Pakistan, create emergencies on a huge scale. Roads and railway lines are often blocked or destroyed and telephone connections lost, so relief workers face enormous difficulties. The first international relief workers to arrive specialize in rescuing people from collapsed buildings, flooded villages, or caved-in tunnels.

The United Nations has helped with emergencies since it was founded in 1945. Several of its own agencies, including the World Health Organization, have two roles:

- Providing long-term aid and training so countries can improve living conditions and develop;
- Sending in teams to deal with natural or man-made emergencies (such as wars or industrial accidents).

# Coordinating Relief

If no outside help arrived at the scene of a natural disaster, the consequences would be terrible. A wide range of different organizations are pledged to help in emergencies, but problems would arise if all these groups stood back, assuming the others would handle things.

Other problems could arise if several different organizations arrived at the scene of a disaster with exactly the same supplies. In 1992, the United Nations established the Inter-Agency Standing Committee (IASC) to prevent these problems from arising. The IASC respects the background and efforts of the 17 organizations (including the World Health Organization) that attend its meetings and help to guide its actions.

The main aim of the IASC is to make sure that the right type of aid and relief reaches a disaster zone. It ensures that no disaster slips through the net and misses out on early relief, or ends up with the wrong type of relief supplies.

The World Health Organization adds an extra element to the second role. As well as helping affected regions react to disasters, it keeps track of likely outbreaks of fast-spreading diseases.

*Pakistani doctors examine an injured man in a makeshift hospital in Bagh, October 2005. A major earthquake caused enormous damage and loss of life in eastern Pakistan.*

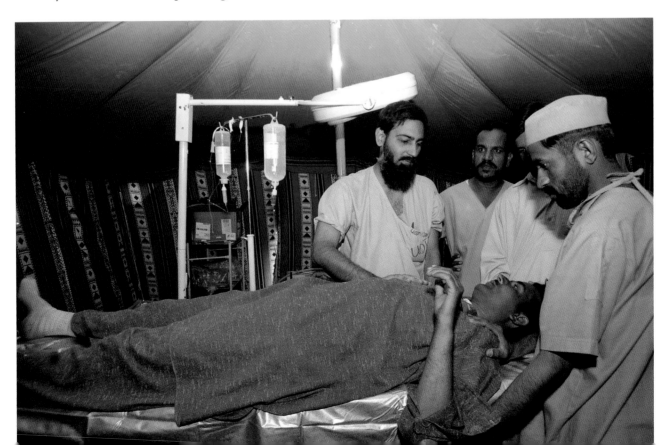

*American doctors were part of the international relief effort that the WHO helped to organize after the 2004 tsunami in the Indian Ocean. These doctors are caring for a mother in Sri Lanka.*

## ... ON THE SCENE ... ON THE SCENE ... ON THE SCENE ...

### When the Bombing Stops

*The World Health Organization deals with sudden medical and health emergencies through its Health Action in Crises teams. One of these teams stayed in Lebanon through the period of intense fighting between the Israeli defense force and anti-Israeli Hizbollah forces during July and August 2006.*

*Doctor Ala Alwan was the senior WHO official in charge of the Health Action in Crises team in Lebanon. Throughout the fighting, he sent WHO groups to check on medical and sanitation conditions in the area.*

*These teams checked whether hospitals and medical centers were open and whether staff could work in them, as well as whether there were supplies of water, fuel, sanitation supplies, and medicines.*

*The results were alarming, showing that Lebanon would face a serious medical crisis even after the fighting stopped in August. Dr. Alwan stressed that the real medical fight had only just begun and that the world needed to help the country rebuild its medical heart: "People are especially vulnerable now, as many have lost their homes and livelihoods."*

# Detecting Disease

A hurricane, earthquake, or flood can have many health-related consequences. The WHO Health Action in Crises teams (see box left) concentrate on the immediate problems caused by a disaster.

Bad as these problems are, they are confined to the affected area. A schoolgirl in Brazil, for example, will not suffer because people have broken their arms in a Chinese earthquake. A sudden outbreak of a disease, however, can send shock waves around the world very quickly. Some of the worst pandemics in history had a single source. Identifying that source—and isolating the disease—could have contained the spread and saved millions of lives.

The Global Outbreak Alert and Response Network (GOARN) is organized and overseen by the WHO. The network aims to:
• combat the international spread of outbreaks;
• ensure that appropriate technical assistance reaches affected states rapidly;
• contribute to long-term epidemic preparedness and capacity building.

*Medical workers must attend to the dead as well as the living to prevent epidemics. These doctors are examining Thai victims of the 2004 tsunami.*

## WHAT DO YOU THINK?

### One Organization?

*The Inter-Agency Standing Committee (IASC) tries to ensure that international organizations do not duplicate each other's work or miss something important. Do you think the world would be better off if some of these organizations no longer existed and the United Nations handled everything?*

# Helping Hands

**When someone** breaks a bone, he or she goes to the emergency room of a hospital and is treated by a doctor, an X-ray technician, one or more nurses, and possibly a bone specialist.

The teamwork of these medical people helps to get the bone on the road to recovery. This type of teamwork—on a much larger scale—is also needed to help with health matters in a region, country, or across the world.

*A midwife, trained to help women give birth, examines a mother-to-be in western India. The WHO supports traditional health techniques around the world.*

The World Health Organization is one of the leading members of this health team, but it relies on teamwork to achieve much of its success. The teamwork includes cooperation within the WHO itself and also with other individuals and organizations.

The WHO collects and processes enormous amounts of information from around the world on health, emergencies, medical techniques, and other subjects. WHO publications range from leaflets to documents hundreds of pages long.

## ... ON THE SCENE ... ON THE SCENE ... ON THE SCENE ...

### Spreading the Word

Organizations such as the WHO need publicity as much as commercial companies that produce cars or CDs. Spreading the word about health not only helps the WHO, it can also save lives.

The World Health Organization calls on famous people or groups of people to help promote its message. They are called goodwill ambassadors. In late 2006, the WHO had the following goodwill ambassadors:
• The Vienna Philharmonic Orchestra (Austria): promoting general WHO aims;
• Sylvie Vartan (Bulgaria): promoting mother and child health in Europe;
• Yohei Sasakawa (Japan): eliminating leprosy;

• Liya Kebede (Ethiopia): maternal, newborn babies, and child health.

On October 21, 2005, Liya Kebede, a model who has been an ambassador since 2005, received the UN Day Award for her work with the WHO. In her speech, she highlighted many of her concerns as a goodwill ambassador:

"Every day we hear about the dangers of cancer, heart disease, and AIDS. But how many of us realize that, in much of the world, the act of giving life to a child is still the biggest killer of women of child-bearing age? That over half a million die every year? Or that three million babies are stillborn? Or that another four million die during the first weeks of life?"

# Teaming up to Help

Every year more than ten million children from poorer countries die before they reach their fifth birthday. Seven million of these deaths occur because of five preventable conditions:

• pneumonia
• diarrhea
• malaria
• measles
• malnutrition

Since 1992, the WHO and the United Nations Children's Fund (UNICEF) have used a strategy called Integrated Management of Childhood Illness (IMCI) to reduce these deaths. The IMCI approach looks at the overall health of a child and doesn't wait until he or she becomes ill.

IMCI experts help health officials to train medical staff in the new method. These teams look for signs of more than one illness at the same time, and don't simply concentrate on one of them. With the right teaching and medicines, they can also offer treatment that helps cure one illness while preventing others from developing.

IMCI teams also help countries and regions improve the way in which they teach people about health risks and hygiene. They make sure people know about protective items such as mosquito nets (to combat malaria) or teach them how to build better stoves (to reduce the risk of breathing-related ailments).

All this training takes time and money, so it is not surprising that some countries lag behind others in setting up IMCI practices. By early 2006, some eastern Mediterranean countries had made good progress in putting IMCI systems in place in most areas, such as Djibouti (100 percent of the country), Iran (94 percent), and Egypt (70 percent). Other countries were still far behind, including Sudan (34 percent), Yemen (26 percent) and Pakistan (6 percent).

*The WHO supports other organizations in the field. This baby in Niger is weighed and examined in a clinic run by Médecins Sans Frontières (Doctors Without Borders).*

One of the WHO's most important publications is the annual World Health Report. Every year, WHO experts focus on a particular health issue. Overall, the reports paint a picture of a changing world, but, more importantly, they help health officials in individual countries to identify problems before they occur.

*This nurse's syringe contains vital medicine for this child in a Zambian clinic. The village clinic is part of a WHO-supported, self-help medical program.*

**WHAT DO YOU THINK?**

### Who Should Lead?

*Should the World Health Organization be taking more of a leading role in educating people about disease and health, or should individual governments be responsible for this in the future?*

# Looking Ahead

**Every organization** needs to prepare for the future, but preparation is especially vital for any group dealing with health. Technology is advancing very quickly in this cyber age, but diseases are also changing their nature and covering their tracks.

The WHO needs to keep tracking diseases such as SARS and avian flu, while at the same time remaining firm about spreading health messages on issues such as smoking and diet.

To accomplish these goals, the World Health Organization is looking for new ways to gather and process urgent information on diseases, and finding ways to make member countries act on WHO advice. The Strategic Health Operations Center at the WHO's Geneva headquarters uses the latest technology to coordinate information and advice about outbreaks of disease and other emergencies.

*An anti-AIDS rally in the Kenyan capital, Nairobi,*
*helped to mark World AIDS Day on December 1, 2003.*

## New Partnerships

For years, governments and organizations such as the World Health Organization (a non-governmental organization, or NGO) worked on their own. People believed that governments and NGOs should avoid private companies because of their aim of making money for themselves.

That thinking has changed. Many people now see how the private (profit-making) and public (governments and NGOs) sectors can work together, to the benefit of both—and more importantly, to the benefit of the wider world.

Private research and funding can boost the amount of affordable medicine and equipment that governments and NGOs can use. Just think of the worldwide search to find a cure for HIV/AIDS. Do people really want that search to be a competition?

Providing health care is expensive, especially for governments of poorer countries. If private companies can share that cost and at the same time work within the system set up by a government, who can really complain?

# Persistent Problems

Despite the many successes of the World Health Organization, health-related issues continue to threaten the people of the world.

• Every year, more than ten million children die from preventable diseases.

• Deaths from malaria average a million a year worldwide and could double in the next 20 years.

• Around the world, 42 million people live with HIV/AIDS; 39 million of them are in developing countries and three-quarters of them are in sub-Saharan Africa.

• More children died from diarrhea-related diseases during the 1990s than all the people killed in wars and conflicts since 1945.

These are some of the obstacles and challenges the WHO and other health organizations face. They also realize that some huge health problems —notably the flu pandemic of 1918–19 and the rapid rise of HIV/AIDS during the 1980s—are unexpected and seem to come from nowhere. Predicting the unpredictable is always hard, but the World Health Organization views that as part of its day-to-day responsibilities.

Since 2007, the WHO has used strengthened international health regulations to force countries to take specific steps to reduce the risk of disease and to report the progress of any outbreak. Better still, from the WHO's point of view, is that their officials can make spot checks to ensure that countries are fulfilling their responsibilities.

*Opposite page*
*A child in Mozambique plays in a puddle after floods swept across the country in 2000. Pools of water breed diseases in tropical countries.*

*Right*
*Hong Kong ambulance staff wear protective masks when there is a risk of fast-spreading diseases such as SARS.*

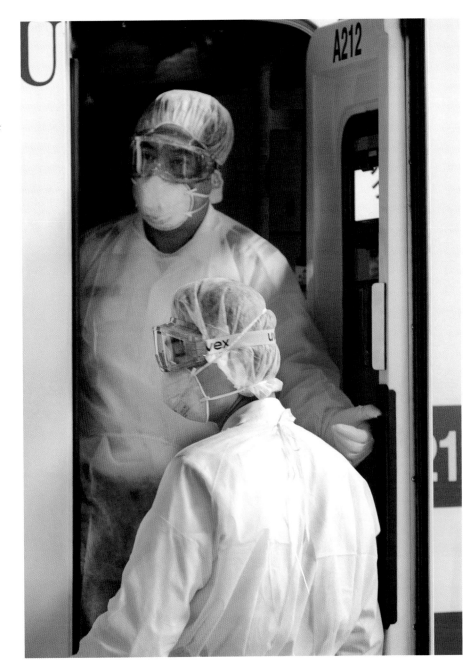

## WHAT DO YOU THINK?

### Uneasy partners?
*Should international organizations such as the WHO become partners with private companies, which exist mainly to earn money and make a profit?*

# ... ON THE SCENE ... ON THE SCENE ... ON THE SCENE ...

## Medicine for the Future?

*Until the 1990s, pharmaceutical companies developed medicines with the aim of selling them for a profit. During that decade, a pharmaceutical research scientist, Dr. Victoria Hale, came up with a different idea: why not set up a company that would base decisions about what to produce and how to distribute it on need, rather than profit?*

*In 2000, Dr. Hale established OneWorld Health, the first non-profit pharmaceutical company in the world. She had the cooperation of other scientists, the Bill & Melinda Gates Foundation, universities, the WHO, and other NGOs. OneWorld develops and distributes medicines to fight many of the illnesses that plague developing countries and enables other non-profit groups to produce the same medicines.*

*August 2006 saw an important milestone: the government of India approved the use of OneWorld medicine to treat visceral leishmaniasis (VL), a disease that kills about half a million people every year across the world. OneWorld scientists are now concentrating on treatments for malaria.*

*OneWorld Health founder Victoria Hale was shocked to find that many medicines had been taken away from pharmacies because they did not make enough money for the pharmaceutical companies.*

# WHO and You

## The World Health Organization,

like other UN agencies, has a wide-ranging goal: to tackle health issues around the world. Some people consider international organizations to be soulless, with nothing to offer individuals. The truth is very different.

*The American Red Cross rushed donated blood from a processing center in Tulsa to help 9/11 victims just a day after the terrorist attack on New York.*

If you have ever put up a poster about smoking or exercise, or if you have been vaccinated against childhood diseases, then you have dealt with the WHO (or the issues it addresses) as an individual.

# World Health Day

Every year on April 7, the WHO organizes World Health Day. The event is marked across the world with a wide range of activities designed to promote health and well-being. The first World Health Day was in 1950, just two years after the WHO was set up.

As well as publicizing health issues and raising awareness, each World Health Day focuses on a theme to highlight one of the WHO's priorities. Many young people organize World Health Day activities in their schools or clubs. Below are the themes of recent World Health Days.

**2001: Mental health: stop exclusion, dare to care** The aim was to lift the veil of secrecy that covered mental illness. People suffering (and recovering) from mental illness can play a role in society and should not be ignored.

**2002: Move for health** Health professionals showed how the need for regular exercise isn't just a problem in richer countries. Everyone, rich or poor, needs to exercise regularly to remain healthy or to regain fitness.

**2003: Healthy environments for children** Millions of children die every year because of illnesses linked to their environment—where and how they live. Changing children's environments at home, in school, or in the wider community could save many lives in the future.

**2004: Road safety** WHO activities highlighted all aspects of road safety, from wearing seat belts and maintaining safety checks on cars, to speeding and drunk-driving.

**2005: Make every mother and child count** Childbirth is a wonderful event—the gift of life. But it is also a time of great risk and danger for millions of mothers and their babies around the world, especially in developing countries.

**2006: Working together for health** No single person—whether doctor, nurse, pharmacist, or laboratory worker—can wave a magic wand to make people better. The 2006 World Health Day celebrated the contribution of the many different health providers around the world.

**2007: International health security** Sudden, wide-ranging health emergencies can overwhelm countries and even regions. The 2007 World Health Day—with the slogan "Invest in health, build a better future"—aimed to increase countries' ability to deal with health crises.

Even the most wide-ranging health programs (for example, those that target childhood illnesses, sensible drinking, or eating right) attempt to influence the behavior of individuals.

## Inspired to Act

In 2001, a group of schoolchildren in Larchmont, New York, saw a television program about African human trypanosomiasis (sleeping sickness), a deadly disease that is widespread in Africa. What they saw was alarming. Without treatment, people suffering from sleeping sickness die, and thousands of people in Africa die from the disease every year. The children learned that medicines that can treat and even prevent sleeping sickness are available in other parts of the world, but they are not available in many parts of Africa.

*The Eiffel Tower forms a dramatic backdrop to a road safety banner publicizing World Health Day in 2004. About 1.2 million people die every year from road accidents, and the WHO continues to press for stronger road safety measures around the world.*

The Larchmont children's response was to set up an organization, Kids for World Health, with its own Web site: www.kfwh.org. They were given helpful contacts and advice by the WHO, some drug companies, and the charity Médecins Sans Frontières. Kids for World Health is now a well-respected charity, helping to teach the world about forgotten diseases and how people can help fight them.

## Checking Up before Checking In

Doctors and other health professionals are not the only people who can benefit from WHO information. Anyone planning to make a trip to another country should read *International Travel and Health*, an annual publication produced by the WHO. It can also be downloaded from the WHO Web site (see Web sites, page 43). The WHO advice is vital for anyone traveling to a region that reports insect-borne diseases (such as malaria), infections in drinking water, or HIV/AIDS. This information is not one-way, simply warning people about diseases they might contract while abroad; it also shows that infection is a two-way street and that people should remain responsible and watchful.

## WHAT DO YOU THINK?

### Direct Involvement?

*The children who set up Kids for World Health believed strongly that their actions could teach people around them and even help others who faced the prospect of contracting deadly diseases. Would your class take a similar step? Which health issue do you think is neglected, and which might be helped by setting up a new organization?*

# ... ON THE SCENE ... ON THE SCENE ... ON THE SCENE ...

## Heroes for Health

*One of the features of World Health Day is the WHO's nomination of its Heroes for Health. These are people who have no direct link with the WHO but have made a special contribution to the health of those around them. The two heroes described below show how varied the jobs of these people can be.*

*Abul Kashem transports medicines by bicycle to clinics in rural Bangladesh: "A main focus of my work is immunization days at local clinics. I always get the vaccines to the clinics —come rain or shine. Porters like me helped to rid Bangladesh of polio six years ago."*

*Margaretha Berndtson is head nurse at Koskela Hospital (Helsinki, Finland), where she supervises a ward of 30 elderly patients: "Working with elderly people is of growing importance nowadays. Finland's population is aging faster than most other industrialized countries, and its birth rate has never been lower. By 2050 nearly one-third of the population will be 65 or over—twice as many as in 2000."*

*Margaretha Berndtson's approach is a model for health workers everywhere: "Dedication to my patients' well-being is my top priority. It's what makes working so worthwhile."*

# Glossary

**annihilation** Complete elimination.

**avian flu** A strain of influenza that kills birds and could kill humans if its make-up changed even slightly.

**Black Death** A disease that killed millions of people during the fourteenth century.

**calorie** A unit of energy contained in food that the body uses to work.

**cholera** A highly infectious disease that spreads quickly in dirty living conditions.

**civilian** Someone who is not a member of the armed forces.

**constitution** A written document outlining the aims and structure of an organization.

**developing countries** The poorest countries in the world, where farming is the main source of income.

**diabetes** A disease that causes people to have too much sugar in their blood; it can lead to long-term health problems if the person does not receive regular medicine.

**HIV/AIDS** HIV stands for human immunodeficiency virus, which causes AIDS (acquired immune deficiency syndrome), a virus passed on in blood and sexual fluids.

**immunize** To help a person ward off an illness, usually through vaccination.

**Industrial Revolution** A period beginning in Britain in the 18th century, when new inventions changed the way things were made. Machines often did the work of humans.

**infectious** Easily passed from person to person.

**influenza** A disease of the lungs and breathing passages; it can kill if not treated.

**leprosy** A disease affecting the skin and nerves, causing discoloration and lumps, and, in severe cases, deformities. Most sufferers live in the poorest countries of the world.

**malnutrition** Not having enough to eat for a long period of time.

**maternal** To do with mothers.

**notifiable** Describes a serious disease which can spread quickly; health officials must notify the WHO if someone becomes ill with a notifiable disease in their area.

**pandemic** The rapid spread of a serious illness.

**polio** A disease contracted from infected water that affects people's nervous systems.

**public health** Government or international efforts to promote health and well-being.

**sanitation** Organized efforts to keep places clean.

**SARS** Stands for Sudden Acute Respiratory Syndrome, a disease similar to influenza. Hundreds of cases were reported in Asia in the early 2000s.

**scurvy** A wasting disease caused by lack of vitamin C.

**stillborn** Dead at birth.

**sub-Saharan** The part of Africa that lies south of the Sahara Desert.

**tsunami** A huge wave caused by an underwater earthquake.

**tuberculosis** An easily spread disease that attacks the lungs but which can spread through a person's body to the kidneys, spine, and brain, sometimes leading to death.

**typhus** A serious fever that can kill; it is passed to humans by fleas living on rats.

**vaccination** Injecting a weak form of a disease into a person so that the body builds a defense against all forms of the disease (including more dangerous ones).

**World War I** A war fought mainly in Europe between 1914 and 1918.

**World War II** A war waged around the world from 1939 to 1945 in which the Allies fought against Germany, Japan, and their partners.

## Further Reading

**Foley, Ronan**. *World Health: The Impact on Our Lives.* Austin, Tex.: Raintree Steck-Vaughn, 2003.

**Grahame, Deborah A**. *World Health Organization.* Milwaukee: World Almanac, 2004.

**Karner, Julie**. *Plague and Pandemic Alert.* New York: Crabtree, 2005.

**Senker, Cath**. *World Health Organization.* Chicago: Raintree, 2004.

**Smith, Roger**. *Humanitarian Relief Operations: Lending a Helping Hand.* Broomall, Penn.: Mason Crest, 2006.

## Web sites

### Children, HIV and AIDS

http://www.avert.org/children.htm

This Web site profiles the impact of HIV/AIDS on children around the world.

### Diseases and Conditions

http://www.cdc.gov/DiseasesConditions/

The Web site of the Centers for Disease Control and Prevention lists the causes of and treatments for the world's illnesses, from avian flu to tuberculosis.

### Health Care in the Developing World

http://world.phrma.org

This informative Web site highlights health concerns and care in developing countries.

### World Health Organization

http://www.who.int/en/

The main WHO site is the best place to learn about the organization and its activities.

# Index